A Century of Silence

100 things people don't talk about

Mehek Jain

BookLeaf
Publishing

Presentation by *BookLeaf Publishing*

Web: www.bookleafpub.com

E-mail: info@bookleafpub.com

ISBN: 9789360941109

First edition 2024

*To the woman who cared for my silent stars,
within these pages they ignite, constellations of
secrets that would never have shone,
without your love and might,
Mom.*

PREFACE

Welcome to "A Century of Silence," a collection of poetry that delves into the unspoken corners of our lives. In these verses, I explore 100 topics often left untouched, inviting readers to contemplate the aspects of our existence that linger in the shadows.

Poetry has the power to illuminate the obscured and give voice to the muted. This collection aims to do just that, addressing subjects that often go unnoticed or unspoken in our daily conversations. From the mundane to the profound, these poems offer a reflection on the human experience, unadorned and direct.

Each piece in this collection is a snapshot, capturing a moment, a feeling, or a thought that may have been brushed aside or deemed too taboo. My intention is not to embellish but to present these facets of life with clarity and sincerity.

As you journey through these pages, I encourage you to confront the silence that surrounds these topics and find resonance in the shared experiences we often overlook. Let these poems serve as a bridge between the unsaid and the acknowledged, fostering a connection between the poet and the reader in the shared exploration of our collective silence.

May the simplicity of language and the raw honesty of these verses resonate with you, offering a glimpse into the overlooked corners of our existence.

ACKNOWLEDGMENT

To my dad, the man who stood for me,
The man who hugged me through all my tears,
Thank you for being my light,
And the warrior who conquered all my fears,
This book without you would not exist,
And I wouldn't have tried,
So, I owe you all these 100 poems,
For you never left my side.

INDEX

Silence

In the depths of silence,
where longing resides,
Lie the unspoken words,
the secrets it hides.

A song of emotions,
softly it plays,
The Song of the Heart,
in wistful displays.

In the warmth of yearning,
where souls entwine,
Whispers are lost,
like fragments of time.

The eyes are windows,
to the unspoken tales,
Seeking solace in longing,
where hope prevails.

In the hushed corridors,
of unspoken desires,
Passions aflame,
like untamed fires.

The heart yearns to speak,
to set free its voice,
But the fear of rejection,
it leaves little choice.

The unsaid words float,
like petals adrift,
In the vast expanse of the soul,
they sift.

Each syllable unspoken,
a burden to bear,
Weighted with longing,
in the silent air.

Yet, in the realm of longing,
hope finds its way,
Through stolen glances
and a gentle sway.

The language of longing,
a subtle dance,
A connection unspoken,
a fleeting chance.

The unsaid words linger,
like a bittersweet song,
Echoing softly,
where hearts belong.

But perhaps, in the silence,
the message is clear,
That love knows no bounds,
and it will persevere.

For in the unsaid words,
there's a language untold,
A tale of longing,
a story to unfold.

And though they may remain hidden,
locked away,
They speak volumes of love,
in their silent display.

A Silent Hue

In the depths of your eyes,
a world untold,
A language unspoken,
secrets enfold,

No need for words,
as our eyes connect,
In the colour that reflects,
emotions intersect.

A cerulean expanse,
like a tranquil sea,
Whispers of serenity,
serenade you and me,

Lost in the depths
of azure embrace,
A love story written,
without a single trace.

Emerald hues,
like a lush forest's guise,
Conceal the passions
that within you arise,

In verdant depths,
a fiery desire,
Igniting our souls
with an unquenchable fire.

Amber shades,
a warm and golden hue,
Speak of comfort and love,
forever true,

A tender glow
that envelops our hearts,
In their radiant depths,
our unity imparts.

In obsidian depths,
a mystery unfolds,
Like the night sky,
where dreams and secrets hold,

Silent confessions hidden
within the night,
A clandestine language,
understood by sight.

And if your eyes
hold a mixture of shades,
A palette of emotions,
like cascading cascades,

Each colour blending,
a tapestry unique,
A kaleidoscope of feelings
that silently speak.

In the colour of your eyes,
a story is told,
A world of emotions
that can never grow old,

No words are needed,
for our hearts understand,
In the language of your eyes,
love takes its stand.

So let our eyes
be the poets tonight,
With unspoken verses,
our souls ignite,

In the colour of your eyes,
a universe unfurled,
A heart of longing,
in a silent world.

Rain and Asphalt

Within the rain's
tender caress,
Unspoken depths
find their address,

Amidst the asphalt's
glistening sheen,
A profound tale
remains unseen.

The scent of rain
on silent ground,
Unveils stories
yet to be found,

Whispers of yearning
and release,
Invisible threads
that bind and cease.

In droplets that trace
their lonely trail,
A mirror to dreams
that rise and fail,

The essence of life's
transient state,
Where joy and sorrow
intricately mate.

Asphalt,
a stage of human design,
Yet in its pores,
secrets intertwine,

A testament to our
journey's weight,
Etched on surfaces,
both love and fate.

The scent of rain
on roads untrod,
Unveils the paths
that we have trod,

The stories etched
within each crack,
Of courage found and
dreams that stack.

It beckons us
to contemplate,
The impermanence
of earthly fate,

To seek solace
in transient grace,
And find meaning in
life's fleeting pace.

Within the rain's
cascading embrace,
Existence reveals
its hidden face,

The scent of rain
on asphalt's sheen,
A reminder of
the depths unseen.

So let us linger
in the gentle rain,
In solitude's embrace,
we'll attain,

A deeper understanding
of our own,
As whispers guide
us to the unknown.

Aching Emptiness

In the realm of my existence,
a silent ache resides,
The weight of your absence,
my heart silently abides.

A bond once cherished,
now adrift, lost in the misty air,
Leaving me yearning for your presence,
a longing hard to bear.

In the echoes of shared moments,
I find solace and pain,
Whispered words and laughter,
fading, yet they remain.

The spaces we filled, now empty,
as silence settles in,
Missing your touch, your essence,
like a phantom limb.

The world feels colder without you,
a desolate terrain,
As memories become fragments,
slipping through the grains.

The weight of your absence,
an unspoken void so vast,
Leaving me adrift in longing,
as time relentlessly sails past.

In the depth of my yearning,
I search for traces of your soul,
Seeking solace in shadows,
where remnants of you console.

But the emptiness persists,
a constant ache in my core,
As I navigate this journey,
missing you more and more.

Moments shared, now memories,
replayed within my mind,
A bittersweet reminder
of the bond we left behind.

The weight of your absence,
a silent symphony of grief,
Leaving me to wander,
longing for a moment's sweet relief.

In this realm of longing,
I'll cherish what once was,
But the ending remains sorrowful,
a melancholic pause.

For the void of your absence,
an ache I can't transcend,
Leaves me yearning for your presence,
my beloved, my only best friend.

Trails of Nostalgia

Within the tapestry of existence,
a symphony does play,
The ethereal sound of your laughter,
in a realm far away.

Its echoes, like gentle ripples,
caress my weary soul,
Whispering of love's embrace,
a warmth I long to hold.

In the depths of my being,
your laughter finds its home,
A secret sanctuary where
its essence freely roams.

It weaves through cherished memories,
silent and unseen,
Leaving trails of nostalgia,
where my heart has been.

A melody of joy,
it carries stories left untold,
In its cadence,
the echoes of a love that unfolds.

Each note, a gentle reassurance,
a balm for wounds unknown,
A soothing presence in the shadows,
where I am not alone.

Like a hidden treasure,
your laughter resonates,
Gently unlocking chambers,
where vulnerability awaits.

Its subtlety speaks volumes,
beyond the words expressed,
A language of the heart,
where emotions find their rest.

Yet, in its absence, a void,
an ache that lingers deep,
A yearning for that laughter,
a longing I silently keep.

For within its mirthful echoes,
I find solace and release,
A symphony of connection,
a harmony of inner peace.

So let your laughter reverberate,
in realms both near and far,
A beacon of light,
a guide through the dark and bizarre.

For the sound of your laughter,
my beloved mother's voice,
Is a gentle reminder of love's timeless,
boundless choice.

Dawn

In the realm where dawn emerges,
A tapestry of dreams unfurls,
Where golden threads of light entwine,
With whispers of a world reborn.

Beneath a sky ablaze with hope,
Two souls, like kindred spirits, meet,
Their hearts awakened by the glow,
Of a shared sunrise, ever sweet.

Upon the canvas of their minds,
Colours blend and spirits dance,
As hues of amber, blush, and gold,
Compose a symphony of chance.

They stand together, hand in hand,
Embracing nature's gentle rise,
Their spirits stirred, their worries soothed,
By the warmth of shared sunrise.

Through veils of mist and misty tears,
They witness nature's grand ballet,
As sleepy landscapes stretch and yawn,
In the softness of a brand new day.

The morning breeze, a gentle caress,
Whispers secrets to the dreaming trees,
And fragrant blossoms, kissed by light,
Unfold their petals with graceful ease.

The world awakens, as do they,
To the chorus of birdsong and delight,
Their souls entwined, hearts intertwined,
Bound by a love that feels so right.

In this sacred moment of connection,
Time suspends its relentless chase,
And they, in harmony, transcend,
To a realm where only love has space.

They bask in warmth, serene and pure,
A tapestry of love's embrace,
As dawn unveils its golden hues,
And paints their love upon the face.

So let us cherish the dawn's embrace,
And the magic it holds within its gaze,
For in the warmth of a shared sunrise,
Love's eternal flame forever stays.

A Broken Destiny

In the depths of sorrow,
I find my solace,
Aching echoes of
dreams unfulfilled.

Oh, the pain that lingers,
relentless and vast,
The weight of longing,
my heart's bitter guild.

Within these hollow chambers,
my hopes reside,
Once vibrant and alive,
now withered and worn.

They dance as ghosts,
in shadows they hide,
Whispering tales
of promises torn.

The ache, like a dagger,
pierces my soul,
Each passing day,
a reminder so cruel.

What once burned brightly
has turned painfully cold,
Like wilted petals,
my dreams slowly fuel.

I reach out,
grasp at the fleeting illusion,
But it slips through my fingers
like fine grains of sand.

The tears that fall,
a testament to confusion,
As my aspirations slip away,
out of my hand.

I yearn for the touch
of triumphant skies,
To taste the sweetness
of victory's embrace.

But fate, in its cruelty,
denies my rise,
Leaving me stranded
in this desolate space.

The ache of unfulfilled dreams,
a relentless tide,
Drowns my spirit
in depths of despair.

The world moves on,
while I remain tied,
To broken ambitions,
a burden I bear.

Yet, in the darkness,
a flicker of hope,
Glimmers faintly,
refusing to fade.

But alas,
it's a cruel cosmic joke,
For my dreams remain shattered,
forever betrayed.

So here I stand,
defeated and worn,
In the prison of dreams
that will never be.

The ache of unfulfilled dreams,
forever torn,
Leaving a void
that no one can see.

In this sorrowful realm,
I find my abode,
Where melancholy lingers,
refusing to cease.

The ache of unfulfilled dreams,
my heavy load,
A haunting reminder
of eternal peace.

Let Go?

In the realm of hearts,
where emotions flow,
Lies the essence of life,
a truth we all know,

The vulnerability in letting go,
they say,
Unlocks the doors
to an eternal display.

Like a bird, timid,
poised for the flight,
Yearning for freedom,
craving the light,

We cling to the past,
the familiar and known,
Yet in letting go,
a new world is sown.

In love's sweet embrace,
we find our ground,
But in releasing the grip,
new strength is found,
For it takes courage

to bid farewell,
To the comfort of a tale
we used to tell.

In vulnerability,
we find our might,
Embracing change,
no longer in fright,

For in surrendering
to the winds that blow,
We discover
the essence of letting go.

A tapestry woven,
each thread a soul,
Moments cherished,
a bittersweet toll,

Yet with open palms
and hearts aglow,
We learn the magic
of letting go.

A river's dance
with stones along its path,
A symphony of grace,
of ebb and aftermath,

In each release,
a ripple's birth,
Revealing strength
in vulnerability's girth.

The seasons whisper
this eternal truth,
As autumn's hues
shed the cloak of youth,

With every falling leaf
and melting snow,
We embrace the beauty
of letting go.

Like petals drifting
from a flower's core,
Love departs but
leaves us with something more,

The seeds of wisdom,
planted in our core,
Blossoming from
the vulnerability we bore.

So, fear not the tears,
the heartfelt sighs,
For in every release,
a part of us flies,

In the vulnerability
of our heart's glow,
We find liberation
in letting go.

Silent Shattered Vow

In twilight's whispered shade,
a fading light,
A silent void engulfs
a promise once so bright.

Bound hearts, once entwined,
now drift apart,
Lost echoes of vows,
fading, as if by art.

Like stars,
that once adorned the night's embrace,
Our love, now veiled,
no longer finds its place.

Dreams crumble softly,
vows cast to decay,
Leaving us stranded
in a muted dismay.

The tender blooms of hope,
they once did sow,
Now withered, lost,
in time's relentless flow.

The winds of truth,
now chill the once warm air,
Silent witnesses
to a love's despair.

The river of our love,
once flowing free,
Now slowed to stillness,
in this misery.

And eyes that
once reflected love's bright gleam,
Now hold regrets
like fragments of a dream.

In quiet moments,
pain and sadness blend,
A love once pure,
now lost around the bend.

This silence, haunting,
in the depths it cries,
A broken promise,
love's demise.

No longer tethered
to promises unsound,
We're left adrift,
love's ship aground.

With heavy hearts,
we must part ways,
In this sad silence,
our love decays.

The Hidden Night

In shadows cast,
where secrets hide,
The echoes of
whispers softly reside,

Through hidden realms
of mystery's art,
They dance and weave,
a clandestine chart.

A breeze whispers
gently 'midst the trees,
Where secrets sway
like autumn leaves,

Their tender hush,
a delicate dance,
With every rustle,
they enhance.

Oh, what tales
these whispers keep,
In twilight's embrace,
secrets leap,

Through the veil of dusk,
they roam,
Seeking refuge in
a world unknown.

In the moon's soft glow,
they confide,
Untold stories
they can't abide,

They yearn to soar
on night's grand wing,
Yet fear the dawn
that morning brings.

The echoes murmur,
softly sway,
Revealing fragments
of yesterday,

In the silence,
they enthral,
The echoes of whispers,
standing tall.

Within their cadence,
shadows gleam,
As spectral memories
take their dream,

Each whispered word
a ghostly thread,
Binding the living
to the dead.

In the heart's chamber,
secrets dwell,
Locked away,
they softly swell,

But the echoes persist,
they'll not rest,
Until truth emerges
from its nest.

So, heed the echoes,
hear their plea,
Unlock the secrets,
set them free,

In the tapestry of life,
they weave,
The echoes of whispered secrets,
they believe.

Nocturnal Shadows

In the dim-lit room,
where night holds sway,
A dance of shadows,
at play they stay,

On walls they waltz,
their movements tall,
The mystic cadence
of darkness' thrall.

Staying up late,
eyes wide with thought,
My restless mind,
a tempest caught,

Sleep eludes,
like a fleeting wisp,
As shadows weave
their whispered lisp.

The clock ticks on,
the hours crawl,
In silent solitude,
I sprawl,

Moon's gentle glow,
a tender guide,
As stars above
in beauty ride.

The dance of shadows,
a silent mime,
A ballet of secrets,
frozen in time,

Each flicker,
a story left untold,
In night's embrace,
their tales unfold.

A lover's touch,
a dream's embrace,
Or phantoms lurking
in the chase,

The shadows mimic
life's ballet,
As I lie awake
in this nocturnal fray.

Thoughts tiptoe
through the mind's terrain,
A dance with memories,
joy, and pain,

Yet slumber's veil,
a distant shore,
Seems to drift
further evermore.

In the stillness,
a world awakes,
In the quietude,
my soul partakes,

Of truths and fancies
interwoven,
In the dance
of shadows unbroken.

I yearn for sleep's
gentle descent,
A sanctuary where
worries relent,

But here I linger,
wide-eyed and deep,
In the dance of shadows,
I silently keep.

As dawn approaches,
night bids adieu,
The shadows fade,
their dance is through,

Yet in the heart,
their echoes dwell,
A nightly performance,
they'll retell.

So, here I rest,
though sleep I miss,
Embracing the night,
its enigmatic kiss,

For in the dance of shadows
on the wall,
I find solace and peace
amid it all.

Seeking to be Whole

In the chambers
of a fragile heart,
A tapestry of emotions,
a delicate art,

An intricate weave
of joys and woes,
Where hidden pains
like shadows impose.

With guarded steps,
they walk the path,
Wearing masks
to hide the aftermath,

Yet deep within,
a tempest stirs,
Yearning to reveal
what pain incurs.

But there comes a moment,
a sacred space,
When vulnerability
finds its place,

In the presence
of a trusted soul,
The fragile heart
seeks to be whole.

A tender touch,
a gentle glance,
An invitation
to take a chance,

To unravel the knots
of inner strife,
And free the heart
from a silent life.

As words emerge,
like petals unfurl,
The pain that long
lay hid in swirls,

The burden lifted,
a sigh released,
A newfound sense
of inner peace.

The listener,
with empathy's embrace,
Holds the fragments
with loving grace,

Together they mend
the wounded part,
And heal the edges
of a fragile heart.

In opening up,
a bridge is built,
A connection formed,
hearts fulfilled,

For in sharing wounds,
we find relief,
A common ground,
a shared belief.

The unravelling
continues on,
Through tears that fall
and fears now gone,

The fragile heart,
though still a maze,
Finds solace in
vulnerability's blaze.

And so, dear friend,
if you impart,
The tender secrets
of your heart,

Remember that
in being true,
You find the strength
to start anew.

For when someone
finally opens wide,
The doors they locked,
the pain inside,

They find a path
to love's restart,
In the healing
of a fragile heart.

Forgiving Shadows

In the depths of the abyss,
I stand,
A soul besieged by regrets,
Unplanned,

The taste of bitter ashes
on my lips,
As I confront my younger
self's eclipse.

Oh, how I ache
for moments gone,
When innocence
danced in the dawn,
But time,
relentless, forged its way,
And dreams once vivid
turned to grey.

If only I had learned
to forgive,
To grant myself
the chance to live,

Without the burden
of past mistakes,
That haunt me still,
as daylight breaks.

To younger me,
I owe an apology,
For self-imposed chains
and animosity,

A tender heart,
yet shrouded in despair,
Longing to breathe
in love's pure air.

Why did I dwell
in self-reproach,
Afraid to sail on life's
vast approach?

I held myself in
judgement's vice,
Denying the beauty
of my own advice.

Through tender years,
I sought perfection,
But stumbled,
lost in introspection,

Yet wisdom comes
with its own fee,
And I've paid
dearly to be me.

Oh, younger self,
I should have known,
The journey's worth
is in seeds sown,

In learning, growing,
and being kind,
To the spirit that
within me shines.

In this awakening,
I now embrace,
The truth that dwells
in love and grace,

I forgive myself,
though late it seems,
Releasing the weight
of broken dreams.

For in the chasms
of regret's abyss,
I find a chance
to heal and reminisce,

To love myself,
faults and all,
And break free from regret's
enthralling thrall.

In this darkness,
a light will gleam,
The hope of forgiveness,
a redemptive theme,

With wisdom earned,
I humbly trod,
Forgiving my younger self,
a step towards God.

Teardrops' Lament

In the shimmering dusk,
a tale unfolds,
A poet's verse,
a story untold,

Within the confines
of a single tear,
Lies a universe of
emotions sincere.

Embodied in
this tiny bead,
The essence of
all hearts' need,

A symphony of life's
sweet refrain,
Yet brimming with sorrow
and subtle pain.

When joy cascades
from eyes so bright,
A tearful dance
of pure delight,

Like morning dew
on petals cling,
A promise of hope,
a song to sing.

But in the depths
of darkest night,
When wounded souls
can't bear the fight,

A tear will trace
a silent track,
To heal the hurt
and bridge the lack.

A tear can speak
of love's embrace,
When parted souls
find solace and grace,

Its gentle touch
conveys regret,
For words unspoken,
hearts beset.

It paints a portrait,
raw and true,
Of dreams pursued
and lost askew,

The poetry
of a single tear,
Reflects the human
spirit's sphere.

Through tears,
we find our hearts unbound,
In vulnerability,
strength is found,

For in each droplet,
courage thrives,
As tears become
our souls' archives.

So do not see them
as a sign of woe,
But as a river
where emotions flow,

In every tear,
a story lies,
A masterpiece
that never dies.

Bound by Love's Timeless Verse

Amidst the shadows
of life's fleeting hour,
I found a sanctuary,
a treasured bower,

Within the pages
of a well-worn book,
A relic of love,
an enduring hook.

A token given
by hands that care,
Inked with affection,
emotions laid bare,

Each dog-eared page,
a cherished trace,
Of the one who gifted
me this sacred space.

As time unfolds
its tapestry wide,
This precious tome
stands by my side,

Its yellowed leaves,
like autumn's gold,
A testament to love
that will not fold.

Between the lines,
I find solace there,
A refuge from life's
burdensome wear,

The written words,
a gentle embrace,
That carries me
to a far-off place.

Through laughter, tears,
and darkest strife,
This well-loved book
breathes timeless life,

In its worn embrace,
I'm understood,
A haven of solace,
where I've stood.

Within its world,
my heart can soar,
An endless realm,
an open door,

A legacy of love,
ever intertwined,
With the one who touched
this heart of mine.

The scent of aged pages
fills the air,
Their whispered tales,
a love affair,
In this sanctuary,
we both reside,
Bridging the distance,
no bounds divide.

Oh, well-worn book,
you hold the key,
To memories etched
in eternity,

For every time
I turn your page,
I find the love
that will never age.

In this sanctuary,
love's essence thrives,
Where time stands still,
our bond survives,

A gift of words,
a soul's connection,
A treasure bestowed,
a love's reflection.

Lost Love

In shadows deep
where hearts reside,
A tale of longing
does confide,

The ache of love,
unrequited, fair,
A haunting melody
of despair.

Within the depths
of yearning's plea,
Two souls entwined,
yet destiny

Denied their union,
cruelly so,
As love's sweet bloom
failed to grow.

A gentle heart,
so pure and true,
With love's devotion,
it imbued,

But from afar,
it watched in pain,
As love's embers
sparked in vain.

The whispers of the
unspoken words,
Like fleeting ghosts,
their hearts absurd,

For one,
the love did not return,
Yet embered hope
continued to burn.

In dreams,
they danced in twilight's grace,
Two silhouettes,
a warm embrace,

But with the dawn,
the dream did fade,
As love's light dimmed
within the shade.

Oh, how the heart
can ache and weep,
When love's affections
buried deep,

And silent tears,
like rivers, flow,
In realms where love
could never grow.

But from this ache,
no strength arrives,
With bittersweet tears,
one never dries,

For love,
though unrequited still,
Remains a wound
that time won't heal.

To cherish love,
both lost and found,
To stand tall
on desolate ground,

For in the ache
of love unmet,
Resides a pain
one can't forget.

Yet, as the curtain
starts to fall,
A truth emerges
from it all,

The ache of love,
a haunting cry,
For some love stories
are destined to die.

So let the heart
find solace, then,
In the depths
of sorrow's den,

For though love's path
may seem unclear,
The ache remains,
forever seared.

In every ache,
a lesson lies,
A soul too tender,
love denies,

Unrequited,
it shall stay,
A love that never
finds its way.

Resilient Scars

In life's labyrinth,
we bear the cost,
Of battles waged,
of dreams once lost,

Each scar a tapestry
of pain and grace,
A haunting map
of life's tumultuous embrace.

Oh, do not turn away
from these marks,
For they reveal
the secrets of our hearts,

In every flaw,
a tale unfolds,
Of resilience,
where courage moulds.

In darkness' realm,
we faced despair,
Yet found the strength
to breathe the air,

Through shattered dreams
and endless trials,
We rose again,
defying trials.

In every scar,
a memory dwells,
A story that
the silence tells,

Each line a chapter
etched in skin,
A testament to where
we've been.

They bear witness
to the battles fought,
The wars within,
the peace we sought,

For scars are not just
wounds of yore,
They're monuments
to what we bore.

In moments when
the world may scorn,
Embrace the scars
that you have worn,

For in their depths,
the truth survives,
Of how the soul
within revives.

No need to hide,
to feel ashamed,
For scars are where
our strength is named,

They hold the weight
of lessons learned,
From ashes,
phoenixes are churned.

Let's not be defined
by perfect skin,
But by the wars
that we have been,

For in embracing
every scar,
We find the depths
of who we are.

They shape the core
of our embrace,
A mosaic of love
and grace,

For in the depths,
we learn to see,
The beauty in embracing scars,
set free.

Proposed

I have a friend,
Who's really true,
There at all times,
Attached to me like glue,

He's there near my bed,
Singing me lullabies,
Laying down beside me,
When I'm gazing at the skies,

But the thing about this friend is,
He's the reason I cry,
The reason I look at pictures,
And let out a deep sigh,

Because this friend of mine,
You can't see him at all,
I call him loneliness,
And he keeps me engaged in the halls,

He isn't a barrier,
To my waterduct,
He pushes at my gates,
Until I've given up,

But the good news is that,
He recently proposed to me,
I think now we're more than friends,
We're bound for eternity.

The Distant Star

Beneath the tapestry
of midnight's embrace,
Where galaxies swirl
and constellations grace,

I stand as a solitary soul,
lost and far,
Yearning for the return
of my distant star.

Each twinkle above,
a memory so dear,
A symphony of light
that I hold near,

I stretch my hand
to touch your distant gleam,
Hoping to dissolve the void,
the silent scream.

You were the North
on my compass of dreams,
Guiding me through life's
intricate streams,

But destiny's hand
swept you to the skies,
Leaving me with memories,
and tears in my eyes.

I murmur my desires
to the cosmic winds,
Trusting the cosmos
to mend what time rescinds,

How I ache for your radiance
to grace my sight,
To fill this chasm,
this endless night.

In reverie,
I glimpse your ethereal flight,
A love unburdened
by earthly plight,

I extend my fingers,
grazing stardust and light,
Attempting to bridge the gap
between our flight.

The night orchestrates
its sonata of dreams,
Within its deep canvas,
your presence beams,

I continue to wish
on each distant star's ray,
Hoping, believing,
you'll find your way.

With each comet
that blazes a trail,
I send my yearning,
my love, without fail,

May the universe
sense my plea,
And reunite us,
in time's tapestry.

Though you've transcended
into cosmic seas,
My hope ignites constellations
of memories,

Until the juncture
when we intertwine,
Where stars converge,
and destinies align.

A dance of aeons,
an astral embrace,
Timelessness etched
in stardust and space,

I hold onto hope,
though galaxies bar,
For the day you return,
my beloved star.

The Arms of Autumn

65

In the arms
of autumn's tender sigh,
A dance of leaves
beneath the sky,

Whispering secrets
of time's embrace,
They twirl and float
with elegant grace.

Hues of amber,
russet, and gold,
Stories of life
and tales untold,

In each flutter,
a chronicle resides,
Of moments lived
and destinies tied.

Carried on zephyrs,
they journey on,
A dance of beginnings
and journeys forgone,

A tapestry woven
of memories and dreams,
Unravelling gently
in nature's streams.

With every descent,
a surrender to fate,
A humbling reminder
of life's transient state,

Yet in their letting go,
they find release,
A lesson profound,
a whisper of peace.

As daylight wanes
and shadows grow long,
The dance of the leaves,
a melodious song,

A performance that speaks
of nature's decree,
Of impermanence,
change, and eternity.

So let's not just observe,
but deeply partake,
In this dance of autumn,
the ripples it makes,

For within its rhythm,
there lies a connection,
A profound reflection
on life's interjection.

In the dance
of autumn leaves set free,
We glimpse the truth
of what it means to be,

Rooted in moments,
yet destined to roam,
A dance of the soul
finding its way home.

Artistry of a Letter

In the hushed expanse
where silence weaves,
A parchment canvas,
where the heart retrieves,

The artistry of a letter,
veiled in ink,
A deeper tale than
what we oft think.

The quill's dance etches
more than mere lines,
A mirror to the soul,
where the spirit unwinds,

Words concealed
like treasures in the night,
An enigmatic puzzle,
a coded light.

A letter's space,
a chalice for hidden dreams,
A river winding through
subconscious streams,

The ink,
a bridge to worlds within,
A secret language,
where truths begin.

In the curves and loops,
a cryptic code,
Unseen emotions
in each episode,

The pauses, the gaps,
spaces of thought,
A universe between
what's said and sought.

A whisper in ink,
an intimate trace,
A sanctuary for emotions
to embrace,

A letter's words holds more
than they seem,
A voyage within,
like a waking dream.

A dance of symbols
on parchment's scroll,
A symphony of emotions
in ink's control,

The artistry of a letter,
a clandestine key,
Unlocking depths of souls,
uncharted and free.

So let the world rush
in its digital tide,
In the written word,
let us confide,

For within each letter,
there lies a door,
To the landscapes of hearts,
to wisdom's core.

In the labyrinth of lines,
implicit and true,
A testament to connections,
both old and new,

The artistry of a letter,
a vessel of grace,
A mirror of souls
in a quiet embrace.

My Father's Guitar

In the quiet hours
of twilight's grace,
There echoes a distant,
haunting embrace,

The whispers of a melody,
tender and free,
A song that once was,
a memory's decree.

My father's guitar,
a cherished friend,
Its strings once danced,
notes without end,

He strummed the chords
with a loving hand,
Creating harmonies
that would forever stand.

But time has shifted
its relentless sands,
And now he's bound
by demanding plans,

No longer does the melody
fill the air,
The guitar sits silent,
in a corner's lair.

The echoes of music,
now a distant dream,
Lost in the rush,
it seems to gleam,

Yet still,
I remember those tunes so sweet,
The memories of melodies
that used to greet.

His fingers once danced
with passion's fire,
Strings and soul intertwined,
reaching higher,

But life's demands
pulled him away,
Leaving the guitar and I
in a silent ballet.

Oh, how I long for
those days of old,
When his music would
warm the coldest fold,

But even as the silence
settles deep,
In my heart,
the distant melody I keep.

I hold onto the whispers
of that song,
In the quietude,
where they belong,

Though he's busy now,
distant in the fray,
His guitar's whispers
still light my way.

So I'll cherish those echoes,
forever hold,
The memories of melodies,
precious and bold,

For though time may separate,
and distance may be,
The whispers of his guitar remain
a part of me.

Flames of Courage

In the fire's embrace,
my soul takes flight,
A dance of passion,
burning bright.`

Its flickering tongues,
a fervent embrace,
Igniting dreams,
a boundless chase.

But listen closely,
let wisdom be found,
Dreams not vast till fear's
voice does resound.

For in the heart's chamber
where courage is spun,
Lies the measure of dreams,
yet to be won.

A dream, unchallenged,
is a mere whisper's call,
A timid endeavour,
a castle too small.

But let fear creep in
with its doubtful refrain,
And suddenly dreams take
a mountainous terrain.

When the dream's vastness
looms like a storm,
And the heart races wild,
aflutter, and torn,

Then you've ventured close to its essence,
my friend,
For dreams are not bound
by where trails seem to end.

The fire that's roaring
within your own core,
Is the forge of the dreams
you're destined to soar.

Embrace the unease,
let it fan every flame,
For fear is the herald
that grand dreams proclaim.

So let it be known through life's
tempestuous ride,
Dreams are colossal,
beyond what's implied.

Only when fear tugs,
stretching limits like strings,
Do dreams find their feathers,
true power takes wings.

In the fire's embrace,
we find our own fate,
Dreams, unafraid,
are the ones that await.

Remember this truth
as you reach for the sky,
Your dreams, when you fear them,
are set to truly fly.

Shattered but not Broken

In fragments scattered,
reflection's lament,
A mirror cracked,
its story unbent.

A girl, who weeps beneath
the moon's soft gleam,
Endures the night,
in silence, unseen.

Her tears like rivers,
gentle and clear,
A testament to pain,
whispered near.

For looks that differ from
the world's design,
She battles shadows,
her courage divine.

Each evening's solitude,
a canvas of sorrow,
Yet through the darkness,
hope she'll borrow.

In a realm where kindness
is often amiss,
Her spirit persists,
an unyielding bliss.

In whispered verses,
she finds her way,
Turning wounds into strength,
night into day.
No victim, she is,
but a warrior of heart,
Turning shattered fragments
into art.

A symphony rises
from broken pieces,
A melody of strength
that never ceases.

For though tears may stain
her pillow at night,
Her spirit dances,
a beacon of light.

Oh, let her find solace
in the stars' embrace,
As she weaves her symphony
with grace.

A girl who cries now,
but will rise above,
A testament to courage,
to boundless love.

Invisible Battles

In the tapestry of modern days,
a tale concealed,
A struggle endured,
a truth revealed.

Women's battles,
quiet but profound,
In a world where their echoes
often aren't found.

They stand strong,
yet sometimes remain unseen,
Their struggles
like whispers against the routine.

Invisible battles
etched into their days,
Yet unbroken spirits
ignite their ways.

In the corporate realm,
they carve their space,
Challenging norms,
pursuing their grace.

Their strength undeniable,
their voices rise,
A testament to resilience
that defies.

Walking streets with courage,
heads held high,
Each step a triumph,
reclaiming the sky.

Not just symbols of grace,
but fierce and brave,
In their unyielding hearts,
they find the pave.

Unheard whispers
of the battles they wage,
In a world that often writes
a different page.

Yet beneath the surface,
determination thrives,
A force that breaks chains
and tirelessly strives.

They are not "too weak"
or easily confined,
Their spirits blaze bright,
a beacon designed.

To lead the way through
uncharted expanse,
As they grasp at opportunities
and dance.

So let their stories
be etched in light,
These battles fought daily,
through day and night.

In unity's strength,
their voices will soar,
Transforming invisible battles
to much, much more.

I Wish You Were My Sunset

I wish you weren't my beach,
I wish your love didn't come in waves,
I wish it didn't stop,
When it crashed against the caves,

I wish you were more,
Than the colour blue,
I wish each day,
I could feel amazing looking at you,

I wish your words,
Didn't have such a salty taste,
And when you touched me,
My eyes burnt with haste,

I wish you were sunset,
Your colours painted the sky,
And each time I saw you,
I would silently sigh,

I wish you were my sunset,
So your love was like rays,
Shining down at me in every moment,
Even in my most challenging of days,

I wish you were my sunset
Because every time I looked at you,
You would smile so bright,
It would change your hue,

I hope you were my sunset,
So I made a difference to you,
Not just one of your seashells,
That adds to your mundane view.

So I'm saying goodbye to the beach,
Dusting off all the sand,
And soaking up the sun,
As I take his hand.

A Shattered Reflection;
A broken Canvas.

In a world where judgments,
stealthily creep,
I bore the weight of their judgments,
so deep.

Not for my words or deeds,
but for my frame,
I turned my own reflection,
into my own shame.

Their eyes, like razors,
cut through my soul,
A portrait of rejection,
my mirror's toll.

Beneath a hollow smile,
my hunger grew,
As I battled shadows,
my strength withdrew.

Each day, I fought in silence,
voiceless, frail,
A prisoner within,
in an endless travail.

The mirrors whispered,
my worth denied,
I withered within,
my essence crucified.

In this desolate gallery
of pain and despair,
I begged for reprieve,
but life seemed unfair.

No triumphant rescue,
no redemption song,
Just a shattered canvas,
Who's been done wrong.

A Buried Ship

I was a ship,
Lost in their ocean,
Sailing waters,
Cold and frozen,

They flooded me with insults,
And I slowly was drowning into the deep,
My silent screams went unheard,
But you heard my tortuous weeps,

You lifted my anchor,
And lifted me from depths of despair,
Your advice came in calm waves,
As I slowly was in repair,

You saved me from drowning,
You bought me ashore,
And you dived back in,
When I was breaking from the core,

If you hadn't, what might have happened,
Still haunts me,
Would I really be floating,
In my own sea?

Or somewhere down,
In the depths unseen,
Where my silent calls,
Are mistaken for a messed up teen,

Your advice meant more
Than you really know,
Instead of giving up,
I'm going with the flow,

I'm slowly feeling better,
Even though at times it stings,
And I feel like a puppet,
Who they play with strings,

I'm slowly feeling better,
Day by day,
And that really wouldn't have happened,
If you didn't come my way.

To My Future Self

Dear future self,
I write to ask of thee,
Did you achieve the dreams
we held so free?

To be the number one,
to reach that height,
In school's vast realm,
did you shine so bright?

The days of toil,
the nights of burning flame,
Did they lead you
to that coveted acclaim?

With books as allies,
did you forge the way,
To stand at the summit,
where scholars sway?

The challenges faced,
the tests endured,
Were the stepping stones
on which you secured,

The knowledge, the wisdom,
the honour sought,
To be the best,
to excel as you've thought?

In classrooms and libraries,
did you persist,
To grasp each subject
with a scholar's fist?

To quench the thirst
for knowledge deep within,
And let your intellect
and heart begin.

Or did you learn that
there's much more to gain,
Than just the numbers
and the fleeting fame?

That education's value
far transcends,
The rank you hold when
each semester ends.

For knowledge is a journey,
a lifelong quest,
A passion that should
never be put to rest.

So, future self,
I ask not just of fame,
But of the wisdom
that you proudly claim.

Did you inspire others
on the path you tread,
To chase their dreams,
to lift their own thread?

To be number one
not just in grade,
But in kindness, in love,
the choices made?

Oh, future self,
I hope you'll truly find,
The balance sought between heart,
soul, and mind.

For being number one,
it's not just a name,
It's about the person
you became.

So tell me, future self,
with wisdom's gleam,
Did you achieve your dream,
or did it seem,

That being number one,
in truth's grand scheme,
Is measured not just by
the grades we deem?

Borrowed Dreams

In shadows cast
by failures of the past,
I find myself in weary depths
at last.

The weight of expectations,
heavy and cold,
Has left my spirit tired,
my heart grown old.

I've chased the dreams
that others thought I should,
In search of worthiness,
Misunderstood.

But now I stand
in the twilight's hush,
Too tired to chase,
to strive, to rush.

The world's demands,
they echo in my ear,
A constant reminder
of my inner fear.

To measure up to standards
not my own,
Has drained the strength
I used to own.

The weight of judgement,
like an anchor, clings,
As I've danced to the tune
of others' strings.

But in this moment,
I choose to break free,
To redefine what success
means to me.

For life's too short
to live by borrowed dreams,
To sail on rivers
of others' schemes.

I'll gather my hopes,
the ones that are true,
And let go of expectations,
old and blue.

I'll seek the light
within my weary soul,
To mend the parts
that need to be made whole.

No longer bound
by others' aspirations,
I'll find my peace
in self-compassion's vibrations.

In self-acceptance,
I'll start anew,
Embracing flaws
and dreams that once withdrew.

No longer hopeless,
I'll find my way,
And on my own terms,
I'll greet each day.

For in the depths of tiredness,
I see,
The power to reshape
my destiny.

No longer held
by others' expectations,
I'll bloom in the garden
of self-appreciation.

Navigating Life

In life's grand voyage,
a ship sets course,
Its fate uncertain,
its strength the source.

Underneath
the endless expanse of sky,
A vessel of dreams,
ready to fly.

Though tempests may brew,
and waves grow high,
This ship sails on,
refusing to die.

For deep within,
a lesson concealed,
Life's destiny,
by our choices, revealed.

A ship, you see,
only sinks when you concede,
To the waters of doubt,
to fear's cruel greed.

Just as in life,
where challenges loom,
Our actions determine
our path's bright bloom.

The sea may churn
with turbulent might,
But within our grasp
is the power to fight.

With unwavering resolve,
and hearts made of gold,
We brave through the storms,
courageous and bold.

It's not the trials
that truly define,
But the choices we make,
and how we incline.

To let pessimism
infiltrate our core,
Or to rise above,
like never before.

In the deepest abyss
or uncharted quest,
We hold the keys
to our life's true best.

A ship stays afloat,
a life stays alive,
When we shield our dreams
and resilience thrive.

So engrave this truth
in your heart and soul,
In the grand tapestry,
life is our role.

It only sinks if
you surrender to strife,
Embrace hope, take charge,
and navigate your life.

Boat

My breath is getting shallow,
I can't find the key!
How long will I be stuck here?
Till I'm finally free,

I'm locked in this tower,
High above all,
I'm screaming and crying,
But no one can hear my calls,

Each minute I spend here,
Feels like eternity,
Anything I do,
Is a minority.

It's terrifying in here,
My eyes are red,
There hasn't been a single moment,
Where I didn't feel dead,

I have tried everything,
Banged on the door,
But no one can hear me,
Cause for them I'm no more,

I'm just a teenage girl,
Going through her "phase"
"She'll get over it"
"Give her a few more days"

I don't need more days,
I need someone to listen,
Someone to scare these demons,
To get me out of this prison,

I'm screaming again!
"I CANT FIND THE KEY"
"PLEASE HELP ME NOW"
"PLEASE SET ME FREE"

Maybe they would've helped me,
Maybe they would've noticed it all,
The reason they didn't,
Is because for them life was a wall,

For me, it was an ocean,
The waves was drowning me deep,
And while they were snoring,
I was crying myself to sleep,

So I hope one day someone comes along
And becomes my boat,
Cause when life is drawing to drown me,
They'd keep me afloat.

A Mother's Love

I told my mother, "I wish I were a perfect
daughter,"
She laughed and said,
"You are as perfect as a sad, gloomy day"
I sighed and asked her what she meant,
She said,
"Darling, without sad days, you would never
know what a happy day is."
"So?"
"So, without you, I would never know what
happiness is."

Time's Magic

Time, an enigma,
slips from our grasp,
Its relentless change,
a swift and mystic dance.

One moment bathed
in the sun's warm caress,
The next, we're searching for a lifeline,
in distress.

Autumn leaves,
once whispered
secrets in the breeze,
Now they drift by, unnoticed,
with effortless ease.

Yearning for a captivating look,
we sigh,
As we stare at their hues,
under the open sky.

We used to swim,
our laughter filling the air,
Now we sit in silence,
hesitant and aware.

In the corner, we hide,
a fool in our own eyes,
Afraid to make a splash,
to face judgement's unrelenting ties.

Once, kindness and truth
were our guiding light,
Now it's beauty, perfection,
in our endless fight.

A chase for A's, a quest for flawlessness,
no doubt,
Even as we rush toward
a burnout.

What has time wrought,
or have we done this to ourselves?
Struggling not to be those
we see on society's shelves.

Yet, amidst the chaos,
there's a glimmer, a ray,
To reclaim ourselves,
and authenticity's bright array.

Let's rewrite this tale,
let time be our friend,
In the pursuit of truth,
let our hearts transcend.

Authenticity, beauty,
in depths of our souls,
The story we'll craft,
as we reclaim our whole.

Salt in My Wound

In the garden of my heart,
I dared to bloom,
Unfurling petals,
inviting light to consume.

I opened up, a fragile,
vulnerable soul,
A trusting heart,
a story yet untold.

But as I bared my depths
to the world's embrace,
I found not warmth,
but a bitter, salty grace.

For in this world,
so often harsh and cold,
I opened up,
only to have my story retold.

The wounds I carried,
hidden deep inside,
I thought by sharing,
I'd find a place to confide.

Yet instead of solace,
I received disdain,
Salt poured in the wound,
causing searing pain.

I questioned why
I ever chose to reveal,
The tender parts of me,
my emotions so real.

But in that vulnerability,
I still found strength,
To weather storms,
and go to any length.

For though some may pour salt
in my open sore,
I'll rise above the hurt,
as I have before.

I'll guard my heart,
but not close it tight,
For in opening up,
I find my inner light.

And as I heal from wounds
both old and new,
I'll remember that salt
can't define what's true.

For within me,
a resilient spirit resides,
Ready to conquer,
with unwavering strides.

So I'll continue to open,
to share, to mend,
For in vulnerability,
I'll always transcend.

No matter the salt
poured into my core,
I'll rise, I'll shine,
and I'll heal even more.

Is anyone really there?

In the silence of the night,
I kneel to pray,
Words escaping into the vast unknown,
I say,

I seek a presence,
a guiding hand, somewhere,
But in this quiet solitude,
I'm not quite aware.

I send my hopes, my fears,
my dreams on high,
But in this moment,
I wonder, do they reach the sky?

Does anyone listen
to my whispered plea,
Or do my prayers dissolve
into the mystery?

I search for signs,
for answers in the dark,
Seeking reassurance,
a flicker, a spark.

Yet faith, they say,
is believing without sight,
Trusting in the unseen,
even in the absence of light.

I may not know
if anyone is truly there,
If a divine presence
is listening to my prayer.

But in this act of reaching out,
I find release,
A chance to find
my own inner peace.

For whether or not
there's someone to reply,
Prayer soothes my soul,
and helps me to clarify.

It's not about certainty
or being aware,
But the solace found
in knowing that I care.

So I'll continue to pray
in the quiet of the night,
With a heart full of hope
and faith's gentle light,

For in that sacred moment,
I can be,
At one with the universe,
with the mystery.

I am but a Flower

In the garden of our hearts,
a longing grows,
Like flowers seeking sun,
our affection flows.

I yearn for a wish,
a simple delight,
In the day's first blush,
and the tranquil night.

You are the sun
that warms my soul's terrain,
I'm but a flower,
thirsting for your rain.

In your morning gaze,
a sunrise so bright,
I wish you'd say, "Good morning,"
with love's pure light.

And as the stars adorn
the velvet sky,
In your nightly dreams,
I wish to lie.

A whispered "goodnight"
as the stars take flight,
Would be a kiss of love,
a tender, sweet rite.

For in this garden,
where our love takes flight,
Your wishes are the sun,
the moon, the light.

With each "good morning"
and "goodnight" you send,
Our love's eternal bloom,
an endless blend.

So let our hearts be bound
in love's delight,
With wishes in the morning
and at night.

In this garden of love,
we'll forever be,
Saying, "Good morning, goodnight,"
Eternally.

Metaphor

In the storybook of youth,
my tale was penned,
An intricate tapestry,
beginning to end.

But the chapters were marred
by an ink so cruel,
A canvas of abuse,
like a twisted, dark duel.

My childhood, a fragile,
weathered sail,
Navigating treacherous waters,
where monsters assail.

Each page of my life a binding,
cruel verse,
A metaphor of torment,
an endless curse.

I was but a bird,
confined to a cage,
A prisoner of pain,
in my tender age.

My wings were clipped,
unable to soar,
Invisible bars,
chains I couldn't ignore.

As I grew,
I yearned to break free,
To unlock the cage,
to find liberty.

But the scars of my past,
like shackles, remained,
A metaphor of suffering,
deeply ingrained.

In this book of life,
I sought a new plot,
To transform my metaphor,
to change my lot.

With strength as my pen,
I rewrote the verse,
Replacing pain with resilience,
a powerful rehearse.

Now I'm a phoenix,
rising from the ashes of despair,
Reclaiming my life,
with the courage to spare

No longer a captive,
no longer confined,
I've rewritten the metaphor,
left the past behind.

In the story of my life,
I found the might,
To turn darkness to dawn,
and wrongs to right.

A metaphor of transformation,
my spirit's revival,
I am the author now,
and this is my survival.

Where did it all go wrong?

From topper's throne
to an average seat,
I once held dreams,
now bittersweet.

Anger wells up,
where did it all go wrong?
In this academic journey,
where I no longer belong.

I used to chase the stars,
reach for the moon,
But now I'm lost in shadows,
swallowed by gloom.

I yearn to reclaim the glory
that once was mine,
To be on top again,
where I used to shine.

But life's currents took me,
a different way,
Made me an average student,
day by day.

My dreams of excellence,
now distant, far,
I've wandered off course,
like a fallen star.

The path to topper's realm,
I used to tread,
Now it seems like a memory,
a dream long dead.

The frustration and anger,
they burn so strong,
As I search for answers,
where did it all go wrong?

Yet within this sadness,
a fire still burns,
A desire to excel,
a longing that yearns.

I'll rise from the ashes,
stronger and bold,
Reclaiming the topper's throne,
breaking the mould.

For even in darkness,
a glimmer of light,
I'll fight for my dreams,
with all my might.

From average to topper,
I'll find my way,
And make the sun rise
on a brand-new day.

Artist

A mother's love,
a silent symphony,
Each note a gesture,
a profound decree.

She's the sculptor,
shaping hearts of clay,
With tender hands,
in her own gentle way.

Her love, a garden,
a lush, hidden glen,
Where fragrant blooms
bloom again and again.

The roots of her care,
they run so deep,
An ancient forest,
in our souls, they keep.

She's the night's sky,
full of stars so bright,
Illuminating our path
in the darkest of night.

Her love, the constellations
that softly gleam,
Guiding us through life,
like a cherished dream.

A mother's love,
an unspoken art,
A masterpiece hidden
within each heart.

In the tapestry of life,
her threads are sewn,
A love so profound,
it has no bounds known.

With every brushstroke,
she paints our life's song,
An artist creating,
our whole world she's drawn,

Her love,
an endless river that will always flow,
A timeless masterpiece,
in our hearts it will grow.

GPS

In the labyrinth of life,
I search, lost and cold,
A human GPS,
my story yet untold.

But the signal is fading,
the screen growing dim,
As I navigate this world,
my chances growing slim.

My heart's a satellite,
once locked onto the stars,
But now it spins in orbits,
lost in space, bizarre.

I yearn for a signal,
a route to my core,
To guide me from this darkness,
to explore.

The destination hidden,
the way unclear,
As I wander through the fog,
gripped by doubt and fear.

My coordinates awry,
I question each turn,
In this tangled web of roads,
I yearn to discern.

Though recalibration
is my desperate plea,
In this maze of life,
I cannot find the key.

The voice inside me falters,
as the night descends,
And I wonder if this journey
truly ever ends.

In this GPS of emotions,
I seek to reset,
But the path I tread is one
that I can't forget.

Perhaps in this disarray,
I'm forever bound,
Lost in the circuitry,
waiting to be found.

The Sandcastle and the Beach

By the tranquil shore of love,
I stood alone,
A sandcastle of dreams,
a kingdom of my own.

But you, the beach, vast and inviting,
I was drawn,
Unaware of the tempest,
the love that would be gone.

Your golden sands,
your whispered words so sweet,
Made me believe in love,
as our destinies did meet.

Yet your salty waters stung,
like tears that never end,
As you became
my heartache's treacherous bend.

In the moon's soft glow,
we wrote our tales in the sand,
But your love, like waves,
slipped through my trembling hand.

And with every rush and retreat,
our story took its toll,
I, the sandcastle, crumbled,
losing parts of my soul.

The memory of your laughter
was a distant shore,
A paradise once sought,
but could hold me no more.

Your salty waters stung my eyes,
my dreams grew frail,
For I had fallen for a beach,
destined to set sail.

As the sun sets on this chapter,
I'll walk away,
Seeking shores anew,
where my love won't betray.

I'll rebuild my dreams
where the tides are kind and fair,
For a sandcastle's love deserves
a love that's always there.

But I'm a Fish...

In waters deep,
where I swim with grace,
A fish am I,
in my rightful place.

But on the bank,
they gather 'round to see,
A strange request:
"Climb that tree,"

Asking a fish
to scale the heights,
Is like expecting day
from starry nights.

For in the waves,
I find my voice,
A world of choice,
my heart's true rejoice.

Yet they judge me harsh,
with sceptical eyes,
As I gasp for breath,
under judgement's guise.

I'm not made for branches,
leaves, or boughs,
In my aquatic realm,
I find my vows.

It's like asking birds
to swim the deep,
A promise they can't fulfil,
a secret they'll keep.

In waters clear,
my spirit unfurls,
In the depths,
I dance with the pearls.

Their whispers hurt,
their laughter stings,
As I flounder on land,
clipped off my wings.

But I'll return to where
I truly belong,
In the waters,
where I'm strong and lifelong.

For judgement's net
may try to ensnare,
But I'll find my way,
with grace,

I'll repair.
I'll embrace the waves,
where I'm meant to be,
No longer judged,
I'll swim in my sea.

Cinema

Life, a cinema screen,
where stories take their flight,
Sometimes I'm the director,
shaping day and night.

With a vision in my hand,
I guide the tale's course,
Scripting dreams and dramas,
seeking passion's force.

In this grand production,
sometimes I take the lead,
An actor on life's stage,
with every role I heed.

The spotlight's glow upon me,
I play my part with grace,
For life's an ever-changing film,
an ongoing chase.

But sometimes I'm a background character,
on the fringes of the scene,
Yet my presence in the backdrop plays a part,
you know what I mean?

In someone else's story,
where my role is to comply,
I find joy in the subtleties,
beneath the starry sky.

Life's cinema unfolds,
with its highs and lows,
It's where I write my story,
where every heartache goes.

And as the credits roll,
my legacy is clear,
For I've been the director, the actor,
and the atmosphere.

So, in this grand film of existence,
where each role plays its part,
I embrace the changing scenes,
with an open and loving heart.

I'm the director, actor,
or a face within the crowd,
Life's cinema, a masterpiece,
Where everything plays a part; each effect and
each sound.

Crimson Stream

In the shadows, friendships tainted,
like a crimson stream they flow,
A twisted path of trust betrayed,
where hidden currents grow.

The bonds once strong, now severed deep,
like knives that pierce the soul,
In this world of backstabbing hearts,
where deceptions take their toll.

The red of trust, now stained with doubt,
a river dark and deep,
Where secrets whisper softly,
like a blood-bound promise to keep.

But slowly, like a poison,
it courses through our veins,
As backstabbing friends deceive us,
causing countless unseen pains.

The wounds they leave are hidden,
like scars beneath our skin,
A battle fought in silence,
where the foe resides within.

In this dark and twisted dance,
where loyalty turns to rust,
Backstabbing friends, like vampires,
drain the life-force that we trust.

Yet, in the midst of betrayal,
we find strength to rise above,
To mend the wounds, to cleanse the stream,
and fill our hearts with love.

For even in the darkest hours,
when friendships turn to strife,
We learn to guard our crimson blood,
and cherish the gift of life.

Dagger

Beneath a facade of warmth and grace,
Lies a smile, a mask, in a secret place.
A dagger hidden, sharp and cold,
Concealed in a guise, a story untold.

The sparkle in those eyes, a gleam so bright,
Hides the blade, poised to strike, out of sight.
A smile that's practised, a veneer so deft,
Yet, the blade beneath, is quietly left.

With every laugh, with every grin,
The dagger's sheen remains hidden within.
It slices through the trust that's built,
With every falsehood, deceit, and guilt.

The world may see a cheerful guise,
But behind the smile, the dagger lies.
Innocence betrayed, hearts left torn,
As the hidden blade conceals the thorn.

Beware the smile that's not sincere,
For beneath it, the dagger draws near.
In its deceit, it plays its role,
A counterfeit smile, that hides the soul.

Caged

A caged bird,
with feathers of desire,
Within her prison,
her heart's true fire.

The door stands open,
a gateway to the sky,
Yet her spirit's shackles keep her bound,
oh why?

She yearns to soar,
her dreams just out of reach,
But her fears, like shadows,
their lessons teach.

With fragile heart,
she dreams of the blue,
Yet in her cage of doubt,
she remains askew.

The world outside,
a tapestry of dreams untold,
Yet the bars hold tight,
her spirit's wings controlled.

Her song, a murmur,
once vibrant and free,
Now silenced by the chains
of uncertainty.

She gazes at the open door,
her wing's ascent,
Uncertainty's chains,
heavy and persistent.

Unseen forces,
they keep her ensnared,
In the cage of her mind,
she's endlessly impaired.

But hope, a gentle zephyr,
begins to blow,
Courage's ember,
a newfound glow.

With a hesitant step,
she draws near,
The door of freedom,
she'll conquer her fear.

In time, this bird
will find her strength anew,
With chains unbound,
her spirit will renew.

With a final breath,
she'll embrace the sky,
No longer caged,
she'll ascend, she'll fly.

Reborn

In a world where
day and night are turned askew,
I'm like a sunflower,
lost in morning's dew,

The night's embrace
was where my dreams once grew,
And now,
I face a dawn I never knew.

The night was my blanket,
my shroud, my guide,
Its gentle whispers were
where I could hide,

But in this world of change,
I must decide,
To embrace the day
or cower deep inside.

The sunlight's harsh,
a fearsome, blinding sight,
I long for the comfort
of the quiet night,

In this topsy-turvy world,
I feel the fright,
As I move to a new place,
where shadows take flight.

The stars that once adorned
my midnight sky,
Have faded in this daylight's
ceaseless cry,

In this world where
darkness says goodbye,
I'm lost, uncertain,
beneath the open sky.

In this topsy-turvy world,
my heart feels torn,
Like a night-blooming flower
forced to mourn,

I'm scared of the day,
though a new path is born,
In a world where day
and night has been reborn.

Castle

In the silent chamber of the mind,
a wall of stone,
Where creativity once flowed,
now stands alone,

An endless night,
a fortress hard to breach,
A castle of despair,
just out of reach.

Each brick, a thought,
once free to soar and sing,
Now trapped by doubt,
a captive of the king,

The king,
a shadow, lurking deep within,
His name, self-doubt,
the root of stifling sin.

This fortress,
built of insecurity and fear,
Shields the muse from vision,
inspiration unclear,

But as the moonlight breaks
through the darkened shroud,
A pen, a sword,
can pierce the writer's cloud.

With every stroke,
the armour starts to crack,
The wall begins to crumble,
there's no turning back,

For the heart of a writer,
resilient and bold,
Will shatter the chains
that bind the tales untold.

The ink, a river,
flowing swift and free,
The writer's soul unburdened,
once again, can see,

Through the ruins of doubt,
a phoenix will emerge,
A writer reborn,
with words that sing and surge.

So, fear not the fortress
of creative despair,
For with each metaphor,
a sword to bear,

You'll break through the wall,
set your spirit free,
And conquer the shadows,
your soul's jubilee.

Wines

In silence, I stand,
a shadow in the crowd,
Twines of longing 'round my throat,
they're wounds,

I yearn for words, a voice,
a chance to speak,
Yet silence binds me,
and my voice feels weak.

These twines of silence,
like a coiling vine,
Restrict the thoughts and dreams
that should be mine,

Constricting, choking,
like a knot pulled tight,
My voice suppressed,
concealed in endless night.

I watch the world,
the voices all around,
Express their thoughts, their truths,
their tales unbound,

I long to join them,
with stories to convey,
But these entangled twines,
my words betray.

With patience, I untangle,
strand by strand,
A quiet strength
to help me understand,

That though these twines
may seem to bind me fast,
They'll loosen, fade,
as I reclaim my voice at last.

For even in the silence,
there's a song,
A melody within me,
strong and long,

I'll find a way,
unravel these constraints,
And let my voice be heard,
no more restraints.

With every breath,
I'll weave a tapestry,
Of words and dreams,
a voice that's finally free,

The twines, once binding,
now a work of art,
A testament to the strength
within my heart.

Ticking Clock

In the quiet of the night,
a ticking clock,
A sound that never stops,
a constant talk,

Its rhythm counts the moments
as they pass,
A poignant reminder
that nothing can amass.

Each tick a heartbeat,
each tock a little sigh,
The minutes, hours,
Just fleet by,

It speaks of time,
a treasure and a thief,
For in its unrelenting march,
we find no brief relief.

A ticking clock,
a whisper of mortality,
It measures our existence
with impartiality,

Its hands point to the future,
shadows in the past,
A ceaseless reminder
that nothing's meant to last.

Yet, in its ceaseless motion,
a deeper truth we find,
The fleeting nature of our lives,
both yours and mine,

It tells us to embrace each moment,
make it count,
For in the ticking of the clock,
our stories do amount.

As the clock's hands move,
a gentle, sombre grace,
Let's cherish every second,
in this fleeting space,

The ticking clock,
a symbol of our time,
An invitation to savor life's
sweet rhyme.

I Thought

I thought,
in whispered echoes of the night,
The answers to my questions
shining bright,

I thought I saw the world
with crystal eyes,
A truth untangled
from deceit's thin guise.

I thought I knew the course
my life would trace,
Each step, each turn,
each future's hopeful face,

I thought that love was simple,
pure, and kind,
A bond unbroken
by the hands of time.

I thought that dreams
were written in the stars,
A path so clear,
unmarred by prison bars,

I thought that in the mirror's
steady gaze,
I'd find a self unburdened
by life's maze.

But in the quiet chambers
of the soul,
I've learned that thoughts
alone can't make me whole,

For life's a winding river,
deep and wide,
With twists and turns
where certainty may hide.

I thought, but now I see
through wiser eyes,
That truth unveils
in unexpected skies,

In every shadow,
every fleeting thought,
The beauty
of uncertainty is taught.

Too Beautiful

In the artist's heart,
a fervent flame did burn,
A quest to craft
a hue yet to discern,

A canvas bare, a palette wide,
and dreams aloof,
To forge a colour,
a masterpiece, a truth.

With brushes bold
and pigments rich in hand,
He ventured forth,
a modern alchemist grand,

To blend the shades
in patterns all his own,
In pursuit of colours
that were yet unknown.

He mixed the reds,
the blues, the greens, and golds,
In restless nights,
his restless soul unfolds,

An alchemy, a symphony,
a quest divine,
To shape a colour
from realms beyond design.

But as his palette danced,
it did reveal,
That some hues,
the secrets, time cannot conceal,

For in his striving,
in his endless strife,
He grasped the truth
of nature's hidden life.

As passion ebbed
and vision slowly cleared,
He understood what
he had long revered,

The canvas whispered,
nature's secret song,
Some hues, by human hands,
did not belong.

The artist saw,
within his pigment's trance,
The world's design,
its intricate dance,

A realisation,
like dawn's tender kiss,
Some colours exist
in nature's sacred bliss.

In humble reverence,
he set aside his art,
Admiring nature's palette,
a work of wondrous heart,

The shades of love,
of sunsets and the sea,
A masterpiece
beyond all artistry.

For beauty thrives
in nature's sacred grace,
Not in the artist's strive
to keep the pace,

In harmony with nature,
we must dwell,
For some things
are too beautiful to quell.

Just Keep Swimming

Life's a turbulent ocean,
tempestuous and wild,
Where dreams set sail,
Unaware of the tide,

With every wave that crashes,
every storm that roars,
We find ourselves adrift,
on unfamiliar shores.

In the midst of trials,
when the sea is unrelenting,
And the horizon's obscured,
no signs of relenting,

It's not in standing still,
in the face of the strife,
But in the art of swimming,
we find the essence of life.

Beneath the surging waters,
courage finds its birth,
As we battle through the tempest,
for all that life is worth.

Each stroke,
a testament to our indomitable will,
The strength within our souls,
a profound skill.

For in the darkest tempest,
when the world feels unkind,
We muster up our strength,
leave our doubts behind.

In the depths of despair,
when we can't see the shore,
Our tenacity
and spirit will guide us evermore.

The ocean teaches us,
as we navigate the tide,
That to survive and thrive,
we must not run and hide.

Keep swimming, keep believing,
with faith in your heart,
And you'll weather life's tempests,
no matter how sharp.

Though the waves may toss
and the winds may blow,
With resilience and courage,
you'll conquer each woe.

For life is an ocean,
unpredictable and vast,
And sometimes to survive,
We need to swim away from our past

Hanging on but letting go
In the garden of our lives,
a tangled vine,
We grapple with a choice,
a delicate design,

For sometimes, to find growth,
we must release,
Hanging on, yet letting go,
to find our peace.

Like ivy on a wall,
we cling so tight,
Afraid to lose what's dear,
what feels so right,

But in our steadfast grasp,
we often find,
That growth and freedom lie
just beyond the bind.

The tendrils of our hearts
reach far and wide,

In search of love and dreams
that cannot hide,

Yet in the clinging,
we may stifle our own bloom,
For life's about expanding,
not a gilded tomb.

We hold on to memories,
to fading lights,
Afraid to lose what once
brought us delight,

But as the ivy knows,
as it climbs the wall,
Sometimes, to flourish,
we must let go of all.

The leaves that fall
and gently drift away,
Are echoes of the past,
the hues of yesterday,

Yet in their place,
new shoots begin to soar,
A testament to nature's
wisdom at its core.

So, let the ivy teach
the lesson of the vine,
In hanging on,
we find the strength to shine,

But in letting go,
we embrace what's next in line,
A tapestry of life,
an intricate design.

Hanging on, yet letting go,
a paradox we weave,
In the tendrils of our souls,
we learn to cleave,

To the essence of our dreams,
to the love we know,
For it's in this sweet balance,
our spirits freely grow.

Hanging on but Letting Go

In the garden of our lives,
a tangled vine,
We grapple with a choice,
a delicate design,

For sometimes, to find growth,
we must release,
Hanging on, yet letting go,
to find our peace.

Like ivy on a wall,
we cling so tight,
Afraid to lose what's dear,
what feels so right,

But in our steadfast grasp,
we often find,
That growth and freedom lie
just beyond the bind.

The tendrils of our hearts
reach far and wide,
In search of love and dreams
that cannot hide,

Yet in the clinging,
we may stifle our own bloom,
For life's about expanding,
not a gilded tomb.

We hold on to memories,
to fading lights,
Afraid to lose what once
brought us delight,

But as the ivy knows,
as it climbs the wall,
Sometimes, to flourish,
we must let go of all.

The leaves that fall
and gently drift away,
Are echoes of the past,
the hues of yesterday,

Yet in their place,
new shoots begin to soar,
A testament to nature's
wisdom at its core.

So, let the ivy teach
the lesson of the vine,
In hanging on,
we find the strength to shine,

But in letting go,
we embrace what's next in line,
A tapestry of life,
an intricate design.

Hanging on, yet letting go,
a paradox we weave,
In the tendrils of our souls,
we learn to cleave,

To the essence of our dreams,
to the love we know,
For it's in this sweet balance,
our spirits freely grow.

Thirsty

They say I have a black heart,
They say I don't think before I talk,
But honestly, I'm a crow,
And I'm not afraid to fight a hawk,

It may be bigger,
But its ego is just as great,
And the moment it goes crashing down,
People term it as "fate"

People say it was time anyway.
But the crow in the sky,
Blood dripping from her wing,
Her throat running dry,

Thirsty
They call her
Thirsty
For attention,
Thirsty
For selection
Thirsty
For affection

Yes, maybe I am thirsty,
Because all this time I'm fed bread,
And I wish someone would look at me,
And not wish for me to be dead,

I'm not just thirsty
But I crave it to the extent,
Where blood is dripping down my wings,
And I'm dying to see you content

Content with me,
With all that I have done,
Because no matter how high I fly,
You ask me, "Why didn't I run?"

Just because I'm a crow,
And I say what I mean,
And I may have said things that hurt people,
But hasn't every other human being,

I say what I mean,
Everything I say is true,
Even when I said,
I'd do anything for you,

So I'm plummeting down the sky,
My wings dead,
And for the first time, I see,
I'm the reason your eyes are red

Storm

First it was the rain,
Slowly crawling down the glass,
Then the thunder,
And the lightning at last,

Each droplet,
each thundering boom,
Each strike,
Reminded me of when we shared a room.

The way the rain,
Poured down my face,
And the way you,
Screamed on those days,

And then
One hit
I screamed at you,
Second hit
My face was now blue,
Third hit,
I just spoke what's true,

But truth,
How can that ever be appreciated,

Because all it causes is pain,
All it causes is being humiliated,

My make-up was over,
I didn't have the money for more,
People asked me what happened,
I told them the storm had made me sore,

But to them the storm,
Was a time to sip hot coffee,
It was a time to cuddle with "him"
And watch TV.

To me a storm,
Was a storm,
Moments of chaos,
And moments of harm.

To me a storm,
Was you,
You tried to bandage a burnt down tree with,
"I'm sorry but you know I love you"

That was the day,
I wanted a storm to mean hot coffee,
I wanted it to mean more than,
lightning and thunder scaring me,

So I moved,
And now the only storm I ever face,
Is the one happening outside,
When I'm having hot coffee on those days.

Plant

I'm staring at the sky,
The moon gleaming on my hair,
Highlighting my teardrops,
And just being there,

It reminds me of you,
How you weren't there in my times of need,
I've grown so much,
And you planted my seed,

But a plant doesn't need,
A moon to grow,
It needs love and warmth,
And so much more,

Something you never gave me,
Something you never showed,
Others flourished in the garden,
I was planted on the road,

Others ran over me,
But you didn't care,
You just looked down at me,
You just stared.

My tears for my water,
My achievements, The light.
I guess I didn't need you,
To come out bright,

I am a "plant"
I need love and warmth too,
But I can love myself,
I don't need you.

Funny, isn't it?

Funny isn't it,
how life's a grand charade,
With masks we wear,
our roles so well-played,

In this world of laughter,
tears, and grit,
We navigate a stage
where we all admit.

Funny isn't it,
how love can be a game,
A dance of hearts,
each with a different name,

In the chaos of desire,
we often submit,
To the whims of passion,
a flame so lit.

Funny isn't it,
how time slips away,
Moments become memories,
Day by day,

We chase the future,
while the past we acquit,
Yet the present's
where our true joy is fit.

Funny isn't it,
how dreams take their flight,
In the canvas of night,
they shimmer so bright,

We reach for the stars,
with hope we commit,
To a world of possibilities,
where dreams permit.

Funny isn't it,
how friendships are made,
In the most unexpected places,
foundations laid,

We connect and bond,
like pieces of a knit,
In the tapestry of life,
a treasure, a hit.

Funny isn't it,
how nature's wonders astound,
From mountains to oceans,
where beauty is found,

In the whispers of wind
and the songs of a crit,
The world's a masterpiece,
in every bit.

Funny isn't it,
how laughter's infectious spell,
It breaks down walls,
in a moment, dispel,

In the chorus of chuckles,
we all admit,
It's the simple joys
of life that truly benefits.

Funny isn't it,
this journey we're on,
Through highs and lows,
till our days are gone,

In this grand theatre,
where we all sit,
Life's a rollercoaster,
with twists and a wit.

The War of Words

It started with a conversation,
Just words, harmless chatter,
But soon it escalated,
Became a war that nothing could shatter.

Our voices, once gentle,
Now sharpened like knives,
We threw our words like grenades,
Creating chaos in our lives.

Each sentence was a bullet,
Aiming straight for the heart,
The wounds we inflicted,
Tore our love apart.

Our love, once a garden,
Blossoming with grace,
Now a barren wasteland,
Where tears left their trace.

In this battlefield of emotions,
We fought without restraint,
Each argument a storm,
Leaving us battered and faint.

We used words like weapons,
With no thought of the cost,
The casualties were our feelings,
And love, the one we lost.

But deep within the turmoil,
Amidst the raging war,
We realised the devastation,
And what we were fighting for.

It wasn't victory we sought,
But a truce, a way to heal,
To rebuild what we'd shattered,
And finally let love's warmth steal.

So we put down our arms,
And made peace with our tongues,
No more war of words,
Just a melody of love, unsung.

In the aftermath of the battle,
We found strength in our embrace,
And from the ruins of our conflict,
Love found its rightful place.

Shadows in the Mirror

In the mirror, shadows play their part,
A face that bears the weight of silent woes,
A canvas etched with lines that mark the heart,
With every crease, the inner turmoil shows.

A world that measures worth by skin and grace,
But I'm a garden, wild, untamed and free,
I seek a path where I can find my place,
And let my spirit dance with nature's glee.

Though words may cut like shards of broken
glass,
I'll rise above the darkness that they cast,
With every scar, I'll forge my strength to last,
In the broken echoes of the distant past.

Yet deep within, the pain remains my kin,
A wounded soul, forever lost within.

Pawn

They say life is a game,
Be careful when you spawn,
Cause the aim is king or queen,
I turned out a pawn,

A piece of someone else's game,
Their decisions, my remote,
Cause no matter what I do,
I'm just the net in their court.

I can be replaced,
Removed if wanted,
They can call me anything,
My emotions haunted.

Why? Did I end up here,
What happened along the way,
I can tell you everything,
Starting from that day,

I had a throne,
A crown on my head,
I fell for you,
I would do anything you said,

You said you loved me,
I was a fool to believe you,
Cause life's a game,
And you can get played too,

Just like that you played me,
A pawn in your game,
You need to break everything in your path,
To attain the fame,

You need to kill the queen,
To rule the kingdom,
And I was a filthy victim,
Of this absurd system,

I believed in love,
I believed in humanity,
You took that away,
Now I believe in barbarity,

But it's too late,
A pawn can't kill a king,
But I can make you fall in love with me,
I can be the owner of the ring,

So watch out,
Cause I'm gonna burn this castle down,
With everything you hated,
I'm gonna make you look like a clown,

You would call it "love"
But I don't believe in that anymore,
Cause im not just the net in your court,
I'm the one who makes the winning score.

Dying on the Inside

Tears are running down my face,
I feel ashamed and hurt,
Like whatever you did for me,
I took it all and rubbed it in the dirt,

You taught me to love myself,
You taught me to stay strong,
But my hands are bleeding red,
I did something really wrong,

These thoughts they were hurting,
My head was killing me,
I tried to control it,
But no one could hear my cry for plea,

The knife was right there,
My hands shivered with its touch,
I shouldn't have done it, I really shouldn't have,
But my thoughts were a little too much

Now the blood of mine,
Is running down my hand,
I couldn't control it,
It didn't go as I planned.

I know it shouldn't be this hard,
For someone like me,
In life, I'm always winning,
But now I'm drowning in its sea,

I need help,
I'm sorry I tried,
But how can I be number 1
When I'm dying on the inside.

Soldier

They say life is a roller coaster,
But for you it was a fight,
A battle for your life,
A battle that kept you up all night,

I remember that phone call,
Like the back of my head,
The tears running down my face,
My hope was pronounced dead,

I would call you a soldier,
For what you went through,
Cause your life was a battle field,
I couldn't bear the thought of losing you,

But you laughed each time I called,
You stayed so strong,
You told me not to worry,
You told me this cancer won't stay long,

And you were right,
You fought fire with fire,
And im so happy I didnt get a chance,
To call you a liar,

Your life was a battle field,
But you played it like a song,
Each time life was ready to make you lose,
You proved it wrong,

That's when I found out,
When your life is a game,
Don't take it for an advantage,
Cause others might not have it the same.

Time is a Monster

Time is a monster,
It steals every moment that passes by,
Each blink a countdown,
Each memory a cry,

Time is a monster,
It eats you alive,
One minute your laughing,
And then you're trying to survive,

Time is a monster,
It plucks at your strings,
And when you're ready to let go,
It reminds you of memorable things,

Time is a monster,
And it's eating a part of me,
Cause now the feeling of being whole,
Is a memory.

Murder

I don't know what's wrong with me,
There are demons in my head,
It's their comfort, it's their home then,
Why do they want it dead,

They control me with words,
Each and every time,
When I finally feel in control,
They show me I'm not mine,

They make me bleed,
I cry from the inside,
But I'm just that happy girl,
Sitting by your side,

You ask me what's wrong,
I tell you im fine,
But I wish that was the truth,
I wish I wasn't about to cross the line,

You say you love me,
But then your blind,
Cause if you really did,
You would see the battles I fought inside,

The teachers say this is not your best,
I didn't expect this from you,
But even when I'm dying,
I'm trying my best not to be number 2,

Now everyone can see the blood,
It's on my arms, my tongue and my eyes,
Everyone can see, "I'm fine"
Was just a lie,

The blood is on my papers,
The teachers asking me where it went wrong,
I'm sorry I wasn't perfect,
I'm sorry I wasn't strong,

But not even the best detective,
Could see what I went through,
Cause this murder didn't involve people,
This murder was for you.

Burn

The lighter is lit,
Its gleam reflecting in my eye,
It comes closer to my skin,
I let out a silent cry,

Tears roll down my face,
Why do I call this relief,
My skin is burning,
But it's an escape from my grief,

I'm so embarrassed,
People ask me what's wrong,
I'm trying my best to fake it,
I'm trying my best to stay strong,

But honestly, I'm weak
I caved into habits that cause pain,
People tell me to stop,
They say I'm going insane,

But the lighter takes my pain,
To a completely different place,
Now I can just focus on the burn,
And not the tears running down my face.

Gold

The moon eats a part of me,
Each time it passes by,
I feel broken and shattered,
With each glimpse into the night sky,

The nightlamp shines,
It's currently 2 am,
But I'm still the "nerd"
After giving everything for them,

My food is running cold,
My eyelids are heavy,
I want to get some sleep,
But being me isn't easy,

I'm holding silver,
They turned their backs on me,
Is that all I'm worth?
Is that all they see?

I'm just a prize you can flex around,
Not a human passing away,
Cause who cares if I'm gone?
If I'm gold while I stay.

Blade

His laughter echoes the halls,
But she barely opens her mouth,
He's from down north,
She's from up south,

His jokes are the funniest,
His tests are marked with "A"s
She's an artist,
And she paints with the shades of gray,

He loves the outdoors,
Dribbling a ball each time,
But for her, even three floors,
Is a huge climb,

He has a coat over his shoulder,
His hair perfectly made,
She never shows off her body,
But wears a coat made of jade,

This is not a love story,
Not two souls who crossed paths one day,
It's about their different life choices,
But ending up the same way,

The night falls,
His laughter now a frown,
Her silent mouth lets out a sob,
They're both sad and down,

He removes his fancy coat,
And she removes her coat made of jade,
They both look at their wrists,
Which was scarred by their own blade.

Deep

I wanted to be more than a "nobody"
But my timetable was flooded with things to do,
I felt like I was drowning in a sea,
And no one had any clue,

They asked me, "Are you okay?"
I say, "Yeah, just didn't get sleep,"
My eyes glued open,
As I drowned in deep,

The pile of expectations,
She'll get another "A"
She's so smart,
Her future is gonna be more than okay,

No, I'm not smart,
But I have this craving to be best,
So no matter what time it is,
I will give up my rest,

If that's what it takes,
For an A* on my test,
if that's what it takes,
To come out best,

Cause who needs sleep,
When half of the world is awake,
And who can sleep,
When your future is at stake,

So yeah, I might be the topper,
But I'm also the girl who didn't get any sleep,
Because in her effort to fly,
She started to drown in deep.

I'm not a Canvas

I'm not a canvas,
I can't be painted red, green or blue,
I'm not a canvas,
Maybe that's why I'm nothing to you,

I'm not a canvas,
But you're an artist of the heart,
I'm not a canvas,
But I want to become your art.

I'm not a canvas,
But I do like the colour green,
I'm not a canvas,
But can you make me your scene?

I'm not a canvas,
But you can paint other things too,
I'm not a canvas,
But I want to mean something to you.

Shadow

This black figure follows me,
It copies every action of mine,
It cries with me when I'm alone,
And lies with me, when I say, "I'm fine"

I'm glaring at the mirror,
It wipes my tears,
I'm glaring at the mirror,
It hides my fears,

It tries to shadow,
These feelings of mine,
But not even the warmest of people,
Can keep me alive,

I call this my shadow,
Because our conversations are unknown,
I call this my shadow,
Because it never leaves me alone,

"Why is that a bad thing?"
Well, this shadow is me,
So, instead of learning how to love myself,
I'm hiding it internally.

Maybe I'm the Devil

My hand shivers,
My eyes looking for a place to hide,
The mirror haunts me,
And my reflection won't leave my side,

They say devils are in your head,
But what if the devil is me?
I got the hatred,
And the disgusting body,

I hate me
I call myself fat
I call myself ugly
The things others can't see

Maybe I'm the devil,
Cause I want to kill someone no one can see,
I want to murder someone so bad,
I want to murder me.

Canvas

You were an artist,
You painted everything you saw,
You'd add a second coat to something,
The moment you saw a flaw,

You painted me every colour,
Red, green and blue,
The moment you saw a mistake,
I was a different hue,

My canvas of skin,
Was signed at the end,
"You will always be mine"
Were the exact words you said,

"Try the pink one"
"And maybe the blue"
I wasn't your lover,
Just a canvas to you,

That's the problem with artists,
They forget the world can't be painted too,
It's just that, you are my world,
So I'm ready to be painted for you.

Lazy Waters

The waves crash upon the shore,
The wind howling in my ears,
The salty water burns my eyes,
But it masks my silent tears,

The sand is just like you,
It doesn't stay for long,
For a few minutes it's soft,
And then, I have this feeling that's so wrong.

The seashells pierce my feet,
Just the way you pierced my heart,
At first I thought it was normal,
And then I saw others love in one part,

But they were in love with calm ponds,
I fell for the wild sea,
When they faced a tornado,
For me it was a gentle breeze,

You held me hostage,
I was grabbed by the neck,
Others ships sailed,
But I was held hostage on deck,

You snatched my heart,
And dipped it in salty water,
It came out burning even more,
That's when I decided I wasn't your lover,

So be as wild as you may,
I'm made for the "wild sea",
But I want a sea that will become,
The lazy waters when it sees me.

Betrayal

They say life is a race,
So my laces are tied tight,
I have worked so hard,
You couldn't tell my day from night,

And now, you took a different path,
Ran all across my heart,
The life I spent years building,
Is shattered to a thousand parts,

You took a shortcut,
Held my hand for fame,
I held yours for love,
Our morals weren't the same,

Yours was to cheat,
Mine was to win,
A pure heart like mine,
Fell for your nasty grin,

So now we are on the same track,
You are few metres ahead,
You say I lack motivation,
But I'm on fire because of the things you said,

You run on fame,
I run on never wanting to be sore,
The thing with fame is,
You always want more,

So your fan count may be a million,
But it can drop drastically too,
It just that fans take a little more time,
To get to know the real you,

The buzzer sounds,
I have won the race,
And you are losing followers,
Just like you lost the race,

"Betrayers" you call them,
But they left for what's true,
So the only betrayal that happened here,
Is the one you did to you.

Dear Future Me

Dear future me,
Did you go far?
Did you buy our dream house?
Did you buy our dream car?

Did you achieve all the things,
We were meant to achieve,
Did you leave all the people,
We were meant to leave,

Did you walk into a store,
And say, "Put it on my card"
Is the future something to be scared of?
Is this journey going to be hard?

Did you get into your dream college?
Are you topping like we planned?
Did you finally find the right person,
To put a ring on your hand,

Dear future me,
My days and nights are now the same,
Cause I'm working damn hard,
To earn some respect for our name,

Dear future me,
Did we become everything we wanted to be?
Dear future me,
Did our dreams become a reality?

Perfection is not Real

It's hard to be perfect,
But you were this close,
As close as the spaces between these words,
You were as close as the beauty of a rose,

But the spaces between these words,
They carry a language unread,
We often look at what leaves a mark,
But what about the words unsaid,

Perfection is not by eye,
It cannot be seen by a stare,
It cannot be noticed within a touch,
It cannot be dawned on by a glare,

Perfection is not real,
But I don't know what to call you,
Because with one touch, one glare, one stare,
You made me feel every hue,

Perfection is not real,
But maybe the world can compensate,
Because sometimes perfection,
Comes in the form of fate.

Invisible Chains

Invisible chains
Binding them down,
It's wrong yet, it's the new normal,
Lurking through every city, village and town.

It's taken many forms,
Snatching the light of life,
A darkness-filled void,
It's no more to live. Now it's to survive.

Freedom was a lost war,
People now long every day,
They yearn for a sense of control,
But society doesn't let them have it their way.

Barriers are no more foreigners,
They say love comes for free,
But now the barriers are the loved ones,
And maybe we're just too blind to see,

Or maybe we chose not to,
Our voices are silenced by pay,
Women are sold off like objects,
Yet we wonder why we can't have it our way,

Slavery is abolished,
But I have never heard a bigger lie,
Because to keep this economy running,
It needs to be hidden beyond the human eye,

Humans chose not to see,
Even after the gift of sight,
Humans chose to ignore,
The screams of this fight,

Because it's the new normal,
And everyone wants to be up to date,
So why change the way this world works?
If that's how it's meant to rotate.

Eternity

What is wrong with me?
I wondered, as tears cascaded down,
What is wrong with me?
I wondered, as my smile became a frown,

I seemed so different,
Like the mirror was cracked,
Each line representing,
The day my smile was an act,

A theatre was the world,
And I was the lead,
But you pulled out my roots,
And now I was a hopeless seed,

What is wrong with me?
I asked again,
To that girl who was shackled,
By the world's constrain,

Her heavy words,
Fell upon my ears,
I could hear her sniffles,
And her anger that was stored up for years,

"I don't know," she responded,
As her eyes bat like a barrier,
Trying to back up those tears,
As her earphones played, "Happier"

I felt like her now,
Like there was no difference between present
and past,
Like I finally knew,
What can come, can also last.

So, my heavy words fell onto deaf ears,
The only person I hold here is me,
I could hear my own sniffles,
That I was going to hide for eternity.

Life

Life is not easy,
In fact, it drags you down,
You may be a king right now,
But you can also lose your crown,

That's why my mom always says,
Keep your head held up high,
Cause sometimes the nicest person,
Can be the biggest lie,

Your dignity should be guarded,
And your mind is a castle inside,
It can go on attack,
Because you fell for someone who lied,

Your guard should be top notch,
A dagger in your hand,
In case someone tries to drown you,
You should have a strong stand,

Life is not easy,
But it is survivable,
sometimes your days,
Will be just as miserable,

Life is not easy,
But I believe in you,
So if one person can do it,
I think it is you.

I Miss You

The words echo in my ears,
Yet my heart is bleeding with pain,
These thoughts, they haunt me,
And they're driving me insane,

You said you loved me,
You said you'd always be there,
But right now I have no one to hold me,
When I'm tugging at my hair,

My heart hurts when I think of you,
I'm not doing alright,
My insta is filled with pics of my friends,
But I'm hurting at night,

I hate that you lied to me,
I hate that I said, "I love you too"
Because now when I say, "I miss you"
You never said, "I miss you too"

Played Like a Guitar

It's like my heart is tied with a string,
Tightly attached to you,
And the thing is, you added another knot,
Pulling me closer to you,

My heart skipped a beat,
When you held my hand that day,
I felt at joy, enlightened,
That something was going my way,

The signs and signals you gave me,
Were as clear as the colour red,
You never said, "I like you"
But I assumed that in my head,

But then, I fell for a criminal,
Cause my feelings are now dead,
You took a bloody knife,
To all the moments in my head,

You played me like a guitar,
And I fell for your song,
But this friendship never stayed,
It never lasted long,

I was just a pawn in your game,
Easily thrown by,
So the next time I like someone,
I'll keep wondering whether it's a lie.

Survival?

Maybe I'm not doing okay,
Maybe my demons are in control,
Because the shattered mirror,
Reflects my chipped away soul,

I have this laughter of mine,
That echoes the word, "Fake"
But people are too involved in themselves,
That they can't notice it for goodness sake,

The knives have stabbed my back,
Blood is running down,
My nose is red from crying,
Yet others call me a clown,

I wonder how I can love myself,
When others only see mistakes,
I wonder how I can love myself,
When I have acted so fake,

But survival is necessary,
And sometimes for that you need to lie,
Because I would have been hunted by now,
If they could see through my eye,

But luckily I have these hidden blinds,
That hide my fears,
They swallow all that haunts me,
And bat back my tears,

Sometimes I don't just want to survive,
Because I see others bask in fame,
They don't just survive. They live.
And I wonder when I can do the same.

Overthinking Shit

It hurts when I think of you,
Yet the time we spent together was the best,
And every night when the moon wakes up,
I can't seem to get any rest,

Why? You may ask,
Because your presence haunts me while I sleep,
It reminds me of how I messed up,
And how we were in so deep,

We were way past the kisses on the forehead,
You were now close to bending on one knee,
But then guess what happened?
I showed you why it hurts to love me,

I overthought every message,
So scared it'll end,
That for hours I left you on read,
And didn't press send,

That's the thing about me,
My heart tends to take the wheel,
That's why a broken heart like mine,
Can never truly heal,

I keep opening my wounds,
To let someone else in,
And each time they leave,
I end up being the sin,

Because to love you need,
A heart that's whole,
And I made everyone believe I was diamond,
When I was just as burnt as coal.

Narcissistic

Others call me narcissistic,
Others say I'm mean,
Because I don't beautify their opinion,
I just ruin their scene,

They tell me to take it more serious,
They tell me I'm not the best,
And I agree I won't come out No. 1
If you held an algebra test,

But I can work on my feet,
And I know that I'm bright,
I know I can work hard,
Each day. Each night.

You may call me narcissistic,
Cause I'm aware of what I can do,
But if you truly knew yourself,
You would be "narcissistic" too,

The thing with us humans,
Is that we put ourselves down,
And the moment someone picks themselves up,
They end up being a clown,

Because society has taught us,
Loving yourself is bad,
And anyone who voices it out openly,
Can be well identified as "mad"

But society doesn't have the strength,
I hold in me,
So encourage everyone,
To open their eyes and see,

Love is not only with others,
You should love yourself too,
Because you can only be No. 1
If you're No. 1 for you.

Feelings are a Burden

My hands trembled with uncertainty,
The tears slowly cascading down,
Their gentle touch caressing my face,
And its salty tips stings my frown,

It's like I'm twitching, itching or glitching rather,
Because I have this overwhelming urge to cry,
Yet my eyes sting with the fear,
That that's how I'll be labelled till the day I die,

I do not want to be the rain,
That causes others to hide,
I do not want to be the friend,
That walks towards the side,

I want to be more than these tears,
That are pushing at my gates,
Because feelings are a burden,
And my eyelids are not strong enough for this
weight,

The door slams shut,
The tap running at full speed,
My sniffles turn to sob,
And my feelings are all I bleed,

There's this knife that stuck,
Inside this hollow heart of mine,
And the feelings that were once hidden,
Are now bleeding out with time,

Feelings are a burden,
They label you for life,
So I wish I could murder my tears,
Like the way you stabbed me with a knife.

These Four Walls

These four walls are family,
They have heard my silent screams,
They know of all my nightmares,
And they know of my biggest dreams,

They know more than you could,
Because you caused my tears,
You taught me that love is pain,
And now marriage is my biggest fear,

You screamed like thundering storms,
And the lightning struck my heart,
And instead of giving me this electrical feel,
It burnt me to a million parts,

You don't know of the times,
The pillow was my closest friend,
My tears soaked onto this velvet skin,
As I hoped the screaming would end,

The abusing words are now my thoughts,
They haunt me each day and night,
And now I'm scared that love,
Comes with endless fights,

These screeching thoughts of yours,
They have scarred my hands,
And now there is no going back,
From your endless demands,

Love is supposed to be pretty,
It's supposed to make you feel good,
But these fights they have scarred me,
More than anyone could,

Each day I come home,
Hoping that I'm alone,
So there are no screams,
That add up to the thoughts I face on my own,

These four walls are my family,
They have been by my side,
They have given my warmth,
When I hid my feelings inside,

These four walls are family,
And they mean a lot to me,
So I may never know what real love is,
But I know what love can't be.

Suicide

These thoughts are a weapon,
They murder my every dream,
They bleed onto my words,
And curse me with being a teen,

They shackle my feet,
And I'm burdened onto this earth,
They weave me mountains of responsibility,
And send an avalanche on my worth,

I have trembled,
Like the trickle of rain,
I have been dismantled,
Like a crashed into train,

This world held me by the hand,
But squeezed it too tight,
The world has cut off my wings,
And asked me to take flight,

That's why my thoughts are my enemy,
I wanna murder them tonight,
I want them to bleed,
And put them up to a fight,

But these thoughts they live,
As long as I do,
So it's the murder of my thoughts,
That looks like suicide to you.

Radio

Somedays I just wonder,
What if I never wake-up again,
What if this is the last time I laugh,
What if this is the last time I feel pain?

Life is like a radio,
We need to enjoy each song,
But in the process we forget,
Its battery doesn't last long,

Soon you would hear it sputter,
As the battery is pronounced dead,
And you realise you're now nothing more than,
Just memories in others' heads,

The accomplishments, the successes,
Are all a thing of the past,
And does it really matter?
If you weren't meant to last,

That was the last that in my brain,
Before I hit the bed,
What if all that I do?
Is it just going to be a memory in someone's
head?

But then moments become memories,
And people grown old,
Seedlings become plants,
And bread starts to mould,

Because life may be a radio,
But its battery can die,
So you better start singing,
Before your last goodbye.

Goodbye

There are a 100 different ways to say goodbye,
But I can't seem to find one,
For every time I search my own dictionary,
I come up with none,

And yet, I am a writer,
Words should flow like the seas,
But I can't find a single word to say,
How badly I need you here with me,

So, a "goodbye" is not enough,
Or not even a book can describe,
How badly I want, need, and yearn,
For you to be by my side,

I can't imagine the day,
I have to say bye,
For you were the one,
Who wiped every tear that rolled from my eyes,

And my dictionary is vast,
And my ability is dry,
For I can't find a single word,
To say goodbye,

So, when the time does come,
For the future can't wait,
Know that even though we were great friends,
I can't stop fate,

So, call me each day,
Text me each night,
For I don't want to lose you,
After I lost you from my sight,

I am never going to say goodbye,
For I never want us to be apart,
So, know whenever you miss me,
I'll always be in your heart.

Locket

This locket scarred upon my neck,
This locket with its old rusty hues,
This locket that dangles everytime I walk,
This locket is the closest thing I have to you.

The picture inside, It slightly burned,
Reminding me of the day you went down,
With the fire raging all across,
You painted me with a forever frown.

Now my tears roll down my face,
And the locket dangles with its touch,
I get this echo—Like I can still hear you,
But that isn't much,

I want our late night talks,
I want our laughing till we cry,
But now you are fading away,
And your smile is starting to die,

This locket I hold around my neck,
Gives me a memory to remember,
For I have already forgotten,
The way you laughed last december,

This locket that I hold so close,
Keeps me in one part,
But for once I wish you weren't stored in this
locket,
Instead, engraved in my heart.

Honey-coated Man

You never gave me a smile,
All I knew was your frown,
I never knew how to float,
Cause you taught me how to drown,

Till date, I still know,
How much I used to hate me,
The mirror used to be a nightmare,
For I only saw what you see,

I saw a broken reflection,
I saw a shattered soul,
I saw a broken diamond,
Who was once made of coal,

You never gave me a smile,
All you gave me were tears,
And, oh, how you made me hate me,
As I become one of my greatest fears,

But others smiled when I passed by,
My friends thought I was funny,
And I realised I fell for your words,
Because your personality was coated with honey,

And then came the sting,
And the sensation we all hate,
You termed it as hatred,
I termed it as a mistake,

For that's all you were,
An error I saw,
Cause you made me think,
That I was a flaw,

But others thought otherwise,
For I made them smile,
I made them feel loved,
Like their time was worthwhile,

So, be this honey-coated man,
But know the bees do come,
And when they do sting,
It'll be too late to run.

So, if you can't love me.

I knew you were different,
The moment I laid my eyes on you,
I felt my heart throbbing, yearning and wishing,
But I could only hope you felt it too,

My body would blush,
And I could feel myself going red,
I imagined us together,
But that was all in my head,

I tried to make conversation,
But I always got the side-eye,
And then you would go talk to some blondie,
And leave my heart to die,

I know I didn't look like her,
I didn't have the flawless hair,
I didn't have the perfect body,
Or that honey-dipped stare,

All I had was my heart to give,
But that was nothing great,
And slowly my love for you,
Morphed into hate,

For you never noticed me,
I was just a passerby,
When I saw home in your heart,
You saw the scar underneath my eye,

So love goes both ways,
But you never had a heart,
So if you can't love me,
I'll love myself like art.

Dignity

I always thought my dignity,
Was going to help in every fight,
But for once, I'm ready to destroy it,
If it gives you the power of sight,

I want you to see,
How you are being used,
I want you to see,
How your heart is bruised,

But love can be blind,
And now you have fallen for a heart,
That doesn't love you for your personality,
But instead your every body part,

You told me to keep my dignity high,
But you're slowly losing that,
Cause you are a queen,
And you have fallen for a dirty old rat,

I want you to be happy,
But I'm afraid to see you break,
Cause you have fallen for someone,
Who is known to be fake,

Either way, I'll be there,
To piece together your shards,
I'll be there to help you,
Play the right cards,

So, I'm undoing your blind-fold,
And sometimes the light is too bright,
But my dignity is worth the sacrifice,
If you are going to win this fight.

Memories are a Pain

I have learned to forgive,
I have learned to forget,
Cause memories are a burden,
And they instil in you a threat,

They scare you of the wrong moves,
You fear your mistakes,
Because the memories of your past,
Have caused you to break,

That's why I have forgotten,
What you did to me,
Cause I am too scared that I'll never love,
After that memory,

I don't want to feel those scars,
That adorn my taped-together heart,
I don't want to remember,
They way I was shattered in a million parts,

I never want to feel like an object again,
I never want to be so bruised,
That my heart aches at your name,
And I feel overused,

So, they say forgive not forget,
But I've learnt memories can be a pain,
So I'm forgetting what you did to me,
hoping I can love again.

Healing

My hands are paralyzed,
My feelings are dead,
For these demons have made me bleed,
And bruised my head,

Now I want to be alone,
I want to feel fine,
But these demons have hunted down my hope,
And I have crossed the line,

I have injured those who pick me up,
I have made them bleed,
For I have given them the pain,
That I should have heed,

Now they have been scarred,
With the battles I fight,
And they try to plaster themselves,
Like I do every night,

So my healing doesn't just hurt,
It's killing everyone I know,
But yet, they stand there,
Helping me at my low,

That's why I love my family,
For they show me how to love,
They are ready to bleed with me,
Till I rise above.

Anxiety

Anxiety is a common word,
Yet, no one knows what it means,
They say it is a common "issue"
Among this generation of teens,

But anxiety is not the feeling,
When you dress all wrong,
Anxiety is not the feeling you get,
When someone ruins your favourite song,

Anxiety is when your hands tremble,
And your eyes tear with fear,
When your mind is a hurricane of thoughts,
The moment someone comes near,

Anxiety is the panic attacks,
It's the constant pain in the chest,
Anxiety is NOT the feeling you get,
When you fail a test,

Anxiety is this banging in your head,
And aching in your heart,
Anxiety is this feeling you get,
That prevents you to even start,

Anxiety is not an "issue"
It's a war inside your head,
It's a ceasefire in your heart,
And a word that has just been spread.

Confused

The word "confused" is used easily,
We blurt it whenever we feel,
But the truth is, we never pause to think,
We just let our thoughts take the wheel,

The world would have been so much smarter,
It would have been so precise,
If the word "confused" was forbidden,
An unknown answer wouldn't suffice,

Because this word that we use,
Is just an excuse to ignore,
For when you don't feel like working,
You start to use this word more,

And sometimes I think how this word,
Really helps us in life,
For if we used that word in everything,
Nothing would suffice,

Humans have learnt to grow,
We have learnt to be the best,
And the word "confused"
Has put our hard work to the test,

Cause people now have an excuse,
They have a reason not to,
But if the word "confused" was banned,
Everything would be just another clue.

To My Reader

This is the 100th poem,
And I have almost nothing left to say,
For this book was for the girl,
Who longed to be understood each passing day,

It is to the girl who is fighting,
Those 100 demons in her head,
It is to the girl who wonders,
If anyone cares of what she said,

Right now, your lips may quiver,
Your eyes, a sea of tears,
But know that each passing day,
You are conquering one of your fears,

Sometimes these demons,
They kill your dreams,
And sometimes these demons,
Make you want to scream,

But I hope this book wiped your tears,
I hope you got out of bed today,
I hope you smiled in the mirror,
Knowing you will be okay,

You are never alone,
And I will always be there,
Remember there are a 100 people,
Who truly, deeply care,

So anytime you feel misunderstood,
Do open this book and read,
For sometimes even the strongest trees,
Needed a little help as seeds.

Other books by Mehek Jain

Available on Amazon.in here -
https://amzn.eu/d/bfPbN2D

Mehek Jain

Available on Amazon.in here -
https://amzn.eu/d/fm5waKG

Printed by Libri Plureos GmbH in Hamburg, Germany